ELEPHANT

(The Essential Guide to Elephants for Children & Adults)

By

Matthew Harper

Image Courtesy of 14thWarrior

For legal reasons we are obliged to state the following:

Hi and a very warm welcome to "Elephants".

I'm one of those people who loves to hear about extraordinary facts or trivia about anything. They seem to be one of the few things my memory can actually recall. I'm not sure if it's to do with the shock or the "WoW" factor but for some reason my brain seems to store at least some of it for a later date.

I've always been a great believer in that whatever the subject, if a good teacher can inspire you and hold your attention, then you'll learn! Now I'm not a teacher but the system I've used in previous publications on Amazon seems to work well, particularly with children.

This "Elephant" edition includes a selection of those "WoW" facts combined with some pretty awesome pictures, if I say so myself! At the end of each book, there is a short "True or False" quiz to check memory recall and to help cement some of the information included in the book. Don't worry though, it's a bit of fun but at the same time, it helps to check your understanding.

Please note that if you're an expert on this subject then you may not find anything new here. If however you enjoy hearing sensational and extraordinary trivia and you like looking at some great pictures then I think you'll love it.

Matt.

I thought that before we get down to some of those amazing elephant facts, we might begin with some snapshots, just to get the juices flowing…………………………..

Image Courtesy of Amoghavarsha

Image Courtesy of crschmidt

Image Courtesy of Namibnat

Image Courtesy of Meraj Chhaya

Image Courtesy of elvissa

Image Courtesy of Henry Brett

Image Courtesy of alexanderhamdy

Image Courtesy of Averain

Image Courtesy of kBandara

Okay, that's it for the warm up, let's get on with the game......

Image Courtesy of johnny_automatic

Did you know that the elephant has the largest brain in the animal kingdom?

Did you know that elephants can consume around 500 lbs of food each and every day?

Image Courtesy of Tambako the Jaguar

Did you know that contrary to popular belief, the elephant does not drink through its trunk, it uses the trunk to hold water, then squirts the water into its mouth?

Image Courtesy of nilsrinaldi

Did you know that the tusk of an elephant can weigh over 200 lbs each?.

Image Courtesy of danorth1

Did you know that the zoological name for the African elephant is 'Loxodonta Africana' and for the Indian elephant it's 'Elephas Maximus'?

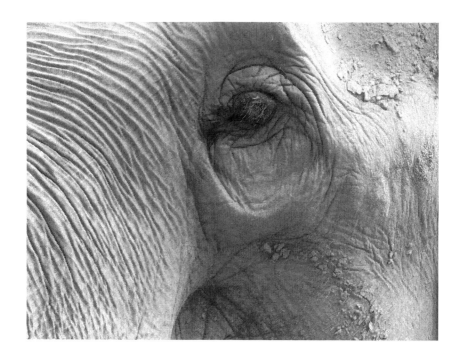

Did you know that elephants are very social animals and live in closely-knit communities called herds?

Image Courtesy of blieusong

Did you know that when elephants swim, they use their legs to propel them along and their trunks as a snorkel when in deep water?

Image Courtesy of jonrawlinson

Did you know that the elephant has been adopted as the national animal of Thailand? They are protected and respected throughout the country.

Image Courtesy of coolinsights

Did you know that in 1916, in the state of Tennessee, an elephant was found guilty of murder and was actually hanged for the crime?

Did you know that elephants are herbivores which means they only eat vegetation?

Image Courtesy of rubber bullets

I'm sure you know that the tusks of an elephant are made of ivory but did you know that due to evolution, they are actually an elongation of their incisor teeth?

Image Courtesy of Tambako the Jaguar

Did you know that elephants are intelligent creatures and have been known to understand a vocabulary of up to 60 commands given by their Mahout?

Image Courtesy of S Baker

Did you know that surprisingly, elephants actually walk on their tiptoes? The front of the elephant's pad is used for walking while the back of the pad, which consists of fatty tissue, is used as a shock absorber when walking on difficult terrain.

Image Courtesy of Ross Elliott

Did you know that the word 'elephant' is taken from the Greek word 'elefas' which translates as ivory?

Did you know that although the elephant is the largest land animal, it has very poor eyesight (due to its small eyes), and surprisingly poor hearing? The ears are large; not to assist with hearing, but act as a cooling system for the elephant as it lives in very hot countries?

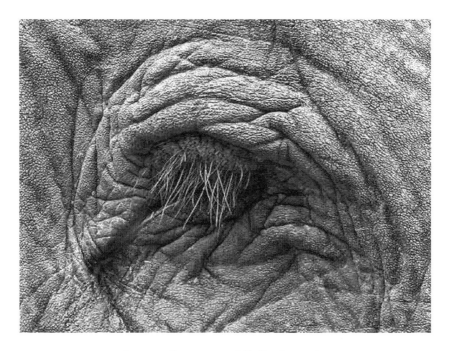

Image Courtesy of Felix Francis

Did you know that elephants have no natural predators? The only threat that endangers their existence is man who hunts these wonderful beasts almost entirely for their ivory tusks and not for food?

Image Courtesy of I Love Trees

Did you know that the pulse rate of an elephant is around 27 beats per minute, which is around one third that of a human?

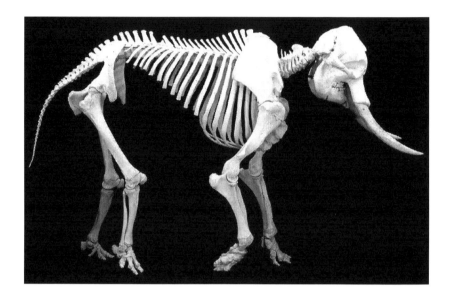

Did you know that the African elephant is also known as the Forest elephant or Savannah elephant depending on which area of Africa they live in?

Image Courtesy of Ana Filipa Machado

Did you know that the elephant's trunk has around 40,000 muscles and can grow up to 8 ft in length?

Image Courtesy of Greg George

Did you know that elephant trainers are called Mahouts and wherever possible, the Mahout and elephant are together for life?

Image Courtesy of letsgoeverywhere

Did you know that elephants are the only mammals that cannot jump?

Did you know that the skin of an elephant could grow to an average of 2.5 cm thick?

Image Courtesy of Eric Kilby

Did you know that elephants commonly wallow in mud or dust baths? Not only does this remove insects from their skin, but the dried mud or dust acts as a protective barrier against the very hot, harmful rays of the sun.

Image Courtesy of Derek Keats

Did you know that the male elephant is known as a bull, the female a cow and baby elephants are known as calves?

Image Courtesy of wwarby

Did you know that amazingly, the trunk of an elephant can hold up to 2 gallons of water at a single time?

Image Courtesy of ZeePack

Did you know that the African elephant can be distinguished from the Indian elephant, not only because African elephants have larger ears, but they also have two grasping muscles at the end of their trunk while the Indian elephant only has one?

Image Courtesy of Chester Zoo

Did you know that elephants have only 28 teeth, but they are specifically designed to grind and chew the vegetation they live on?

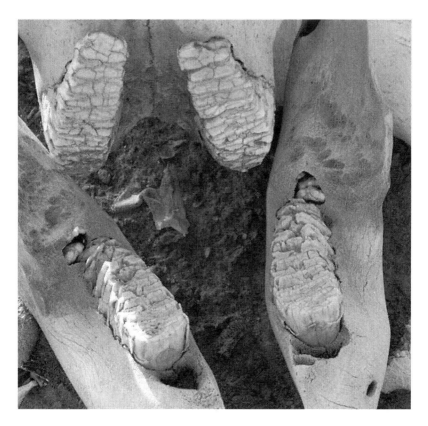

Image Courtesy of Christopher T Cooper

Did you know that the elephant digests only around half of what it eats per day? In order to assist with their digestion, they consume around 30/50 gallons of water each day.

Did you know that an elephant's droppings are extremely high in nutrients and make ideal fertilizer?

Image Courtesy of jitze

Did you know that an African elephant grows to around 13 ft in height, whereas the Indian elephant is only about 10 ft high?

Image Courtesy of TJ Ryan

Did you know that it is extremely difficult to identify the sex of an elephant, as both male and female elephants have few, if any visual sexual organs? Often, the sex of an elephant is determined by the forehead as the female generally has a more pronounced forehead than the male.

Image Courtesy of APM Alex

Did you know that elephants point their trunks upwards and wave them from side to side to smell? They also use their feet to detect vibrations in the ground, to locate the rest of their herd.

Image Courtesy of Tambako the Jaguar

Did you know that elephants signal anger by blowing dust in the air from their trunks? They also rapidly flap their ears.

Image Courtesy of wendylin20

Did you know that an African elephant's back is concave (has a slight dip in it) whereas the Indian elephant's back is convex (has a slight hump on it), so it is easier to ride bareback on an African elephant?

Image Courtesy of permanently scatterbrained

Did you know that male African elephants weigh around 16,000 lbs, but the Indian male elephant only weighs around 11,000 lbs?

Image Courtesy of generalising

Did you know that the female elephant becomes sexually active at around 12 years old? She remains pregnant for 22 months, the longest gestation period of any mammal. Only one calf is born each time, then she waits around 4 years before mating again?

Image Courtesy of alexdecarvalho

Did you know that the front legs of all elephants have five toes, however, the rear legs can have three, four or five toes, dependant on the species of elephant?.

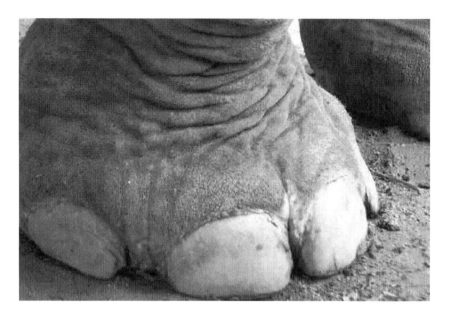

Image Courtesy of kbakar

Did you know that when elephants travel long distances, they actually follow the same path their ancestors trod?

Image Courtesy of sarahemcc

Did you know that in Thailand, March 13th is recognised as National Thai Elephant Day. September 22nd is recognised as Elephant Appreciation Day?

Image Courtesy of unicron1bot

Did you know that both African and Indian elephants have an average life span of 70 years?.

Image Courtesy of MaxH42

Did you know that in some Asian cultures, the elephant symbolizes wisdom?

Image Courtesy of h.koppdelaney

Did you know that in some parts of the world where elephants live freely, the roads, which cut through their environment, actually have road signs warning of elephants crossing?

Image Courtesy of fortes

Did you know that when elephants are angry and stampede, they can charge at speeds of up to 25 mph?

Image Courtesy of Marc Veraart

Did you know that elephant trainers at a safari park in Thailand, taught an elephant to walk a reinforced tightrope? It performs daily shows for tourists.

Image Courtesy of Will Ellis

Did you know that elephants can swim and walk for extremely long distances? They walk at around 4 mph.

Image Courtesy of Risager

Did you know that similar to humans being left or right hand dependant, the elephant is either left or right tusk dependant?

Image Courtesy of wwarby

Did you know that due to its immense size, one elephant tooth could weigh almost 3 Kilograms?

Image Courtesy of Mot the barber

Did you know that in World War II, the first bomb to be dropped on Berlin by Allied troops actually fell on Berlin Zoo, killing the only resident elephant?

Did you know that the elephant is the only mammal which has 4 knee joints rather than 2 knees and 2 elbows? This means that when laid on the ground, all its legs point backwards.

Image Courtesy of generalising

Did you know that elephants spend up to 16 hours a day eating?

Image Courtesy of flowcomm

That's about it for the elephant trivia for now. I'd like to finish this publication with TEN "True or False" questions based on what you've just read. It should help you to really cement the information and to test your memory recall!

....

....

DON'T FORGET TO KEEP YOUR SCORE: THERE'S 1 POINT FOR EACH OF THE FIRST 9 QUESTIONS AND 5 POINTS FOR THE BONUS QUESTION GIVING A TOTAL OF 14 POINTS ....

1.

TRUE or FALSE: The elephant has the largest brain in the animal kingdom.

TRUE.

2.

TRUE or FALSE: The elephant has been adopted as the national animal of Finland.

FALSE:

The elephant has been adopted as the national animal of THAILAND.

3.

TRUE or FALSE: Elephants actually walk on their tiptoes

TRUE

4.

TRUE or FALSE: Elephants are the only mammals that cannot jump.

TRUE

5.

TRUE or FALSE: The trunk of an elephant can hold up to 2
gallons of water at a single time.

TRUE

6.

TRUE or FALSE: The elephant has the shortest gestation period of any mammal.

FALSE

The elephant has the LONGEST gestation period of any mammal.

7.

TRUE or FALSE: The front legs of all elephants have four toes.

FALSE

The front legs of all elephants have FIVE toes.

8.

TRUE or FALSE: Both African and Indian elephants have an average life span of 70 years.

TRUE

9.

TRUE or FALSE: Elephants can charge at speeds of up to 55 mph.

FALSE

Elephants can charge at speeds of up to 25 mph.

10.

BONUS ROUND WORTH 5 POINTS

TRUE or FALSE: Elephants spend up to 16 hours a day eating.

TRUE

Congratulations, you made it to the end!

I sincerely hope you enjoyed my little elephant project and that you learnt a thing or two. I certainly did when I was doing the research. It's sad to know that we are the only threat to the elephant's survival.

ADD UP YOUR SCORE NOW.

1 point for each of the first 9 correct answers plus 5 points for the bonus round giving a grand total of 14 points.

If you genuinely achieved 14 points then you are indeed an "ELEPHANT MASTER".

8 to 13 points proves you are an "ELEPHANT LEGEND".

4 to 7 points shows you are an "ELEPHANT ENTHUSIAST".

0 to 3 points shows you are an "ELEPHANT ADMIRER".

NICE WORK!

Matt.

Thank you once again for choosing this publication. If you enjoyed it then please let me know using the Customer Review Section through Amazon.

If you would like to read more of my work then simply type in my name using the Amazon Search Box and hopefully you'll find something else that "takes your fancy" or go directly to my website printed below.

Until we meet again,

Matthew Harper

www.matthewharper.info

Image Courtesy of 14thWarrior